Praying In The Presence Of
OUR LORD
for
Children

*May God bless you & be always with you.
Fr. Anton*

Praying In The Presence Of
Our Lord
for
Children

Fr. Antoine Thomas, f.j.
Fr. Benedict J. Groeschel, C.F.R.
Series Editor

Illustrations by
Fr. Joseph Mary Brown, f.j.

Our Sunday Visitor Publishing Division
Our Sunday Visitor, Inc.
Huntington, Indiana 46750

Nihil Obstat
Rev. Michael Heintz
Censor Librorum

Imprimatur
✠ John M. D'Arcy
Bishop of Fort Wayne-South Bend
June 18, 2003

The *nihil obstat* and *imprimatur* are declarations that a work is free from doctrinal or moral error. It is not implied that those who have granted the *nihil obstat* and *imprimatur* agree with the contents, opinions, or statements expressed.

Our Sunday Visitor Publishing Division
Our Sunday Visitor, Inc.
200 Noll Plaza
Huntington, IN 46750

ISBN: 978-1-931709-95-8 (Inventory No. T52)
LCCN: 2003105346

Cover design by Tyler Ottinger
Cover and interior art by Rev. Joseph Mary Brown, f.j.
Interior design by Sherri L. Hoffman

PRINTED IN THE UNITED STATES OF AMERICA

"Let The Little children be, and do not
hinder Them from coming To me,
for of such is The kingdom of heaven."
— MATTHEW 19:14

Table of Contents

Foreword

Dear Children,

This very special prayer book is for you! It is written and illustrated by two friends of Jesus. Who is Jesus? As you certainly already know, He is the best friend you can dream of. A true friend whom you can call upon anytime you want — not on the phone, of course, but by praying in your heart.

Do you know what? Jesus, who was miraculously conceived in the womb of the Virgin Mary two thousand years ago, died on the cross to reveal His infinite love for His Father and for us sinners. But He also rose from the dead — because Jesus Christ is GOD! Unbelievable? Yes — but God, through the Sacrament of Baptism, has poured into our souls the invisible gift of faith so that we can believe, hope, and love. So, dear children, by praying, we can thank God the Father for the incredible gift of His beloved Son!

Behold what manner of love the Father has bestowed upon us, that we should be called children of God; and such we are. — 1 JOHN 3:1

Children are important to God! Jesus loves you so much! Listen to what He said:

"Let the little children be, and do not hinder them from coming to me, for of such is the kingdom of heaven." — MATTHEW 19:14

Do You Like to Play?

Of course you like to play! It would be odd for a child not to like playing. But tell me, do you also like to *pray*? Or sometimes do you seem to like your Game Boy, computer, or TV more than God?

Let's make a deal. If you play once a day, *pray* at least once a day! If you play twice a day, *pray* at least twice a day! If you play three times a day or more, then why not decide to *pray* three times a day or more?

Do you like this deal? I'm sure that you're smiling at this unusual deal! But think how pleased your parents and God will be if you decide to lift up your soul to Him several times a day and adore Him as Creator and Father!

> *Isn't it your choice to play only,*
> *or to play and to pray joyfully?*
> *A child plays, but a child of God prays.*
> *To pray is to love. . . . That's heaven's way!*

By the way, what time is it? IT'S TIME TO LOVE!

With this little prayer book, you will find help to remain close to Jesus throughout your day, from the moment you wake up until bedtime.

God bless you, dear children!

— FATHER ANTOINE

InTroduCTion

When we pray for real, and don't just say words to God, we need to use more than our lips. Praying is very different from reciting the Pledge of Allegiance to the flag at school, even though we are sincere when saying the pledge.

We have to use our minds and think about what the words mean, and we have to use our hearts and try to feel the meaning of the words. When we thank God, we should be happy. And when we tell Him we are sorry for any bad or stupid things we have done, we should feel sorry.

Because He came from heaven into this world, and because we can picture Him as a human being, it is easiest to speak to Jesus when we pray. We can think of Him as a baby, as a young man, as a man dying on the cross, and as the King of kings in heaven. For Catholics, it is very special to pray to Jesus present with us at every moment, just as if He were standing by us or sitting in the same room. This is because the Holy Eucharist is truly the Body and Blood of Jesus. He himself tells us that in the Gospel: "I am the living bread that has come down from heaven. If anyone eats of this bread he shall live forever; and the bread that I will give is my flesh for the life of the world" (John 6:51).

Because the Blessed Sacrament, which is also called the Eucharist, contains Jesus' Body and Blood, soul and divinity, under the appearance of bread and wine, we should always be reverent in church. We are there with Jesus, just as if we were with Him in Jerusalem or Nazareth. What a great favor it is to be near Him in the tabernacle, the beautiful box where the Holy Eucharist is kept in church! When we go to pray near the tabernacle, it is as if we were visiting Jesus in Nazareth. Father Antoine Thomas, who wrote this book, reminds us that Jesus is with us in many ways. But it is easiest to pray to Him in His mysterious presence in the tabernacle.

I was very lucky. When I went to grammar school a long time ago, the sisters taught us to pray, and to pray well and often. You may not have that good an opportunity, but this book about prayer can help you a lot. Pray sincerely and you will pray better. Pray every day and soon you will find that you can pray even when you have to do other things. You can pray at the same time. When things go wrong, you will know how to pray and you will remember that Jesus is with you. Just as Jesus was ascending into heaven, He told us that He would be with us always, even to the end of the world. (Read Matthew 28:16-20.) It is by praying that we can be with Him.

— FATHER BENEDICT J. GROESCHEL, C.F.R.
Series Editor

How To Use This Book

I invite you to open this little book a lot, and then you will quickly understand how to keep yourself in the presence of God all day long!

- ⓖ Keep this prayer book on your bedside table. You can use it for morning and evening prayer.
- ⓖ Take it with you in your school bag to use during breaks at school.
- ⓖ You can easily pray before an activity by looking at the list of the thirty chapter titles in this prayer book.
- ⓖ Remember . . .
  - ✕ the importance of praying the Our Father, because it is *the only prayer* Jesus taught us!
  - ✕ that Jesus is with you during the day, no matter what you do.
  - ✕ that because you are baptized, you never pray alone but with the Church and in Jesus Christ!
- ⓖ Out of concern for your classmates, you may show them your little book and share what is good and helpful for them, too!

And don't forget: *To pray often is to love God often!*

PART ONE

To God, My Creator and Father

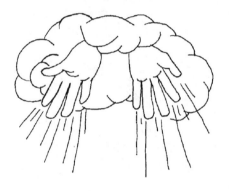

I believe in God, the Father almighty,
creator of heaven and earth....
— THE APOSTLES' CREED

Chapter 1

God, My Creator, I Adore You!

Know That The LORD is God! IT is he That made us,
and we are his; we are his people and
The sheep of his pasture.
— Psalm 100:3

My soul Thirsts for God, for The Living God.
When shall I come and behold The face of God?
— PSALM 42:2

My Questions

- ⑥ Since God is invisible, how can I discover signs of His presence on earth?
- ⑥ How can I ever meet Him and talk to Him?
- ⑥ Can I pray to a God I do not see and do not hear?

The Word of God

Yes, you can! Just take a minute to open your Bible, find where the Book of Wisdom is, go to Chapter 13 and read from verse 1 to verse 13. It starts with the following words:

For all men who were ignorant of God were foolish by nature; and they were unable from the good things that are seen to know him who exists, nor did they recognize the craftsman while paying heed to his works.

— WISDOM 13:1

Continue to read the rest of the verses by yourself.

St. Paul, too, reminds us that the existence of God, our Creator, is manifested through the beauty of the universe He created out of love for us:

For what can be known about God is plain to them, because God has shown it to them. Ever since the creation

of the world his invisible nature, namely, his eternal
power and deity, has been clearly perceived in the things
that have been made. So they are without excuse.

— ROMANS 1:19-20; RSV

Prayer

My Prayer to God

Lord, my God, I get so distracted by many things through-
out the day that I even forget your existence! I'm sorry, Lord!
I want to adore you as the Creator of the universe and the
Creator of my soul. I know that at each second of my life you
sustain my very being. I thank you for giving me a spirit
created in your own image so that I can discover you, the
source and ultimate end of what exists.

Please, my God, give me the grace to live continuously in
your holy presence in whatever I may do and wherever I am.

Thank you, Lord. Amen.

A Friend of Jesus

"O my God, my only hope, I have placed all my trust in
you, and I know that I shall not be disappointed."

— ST. FAUSTINA

Chapter 2

6

Lord, Teach Us How to Pray

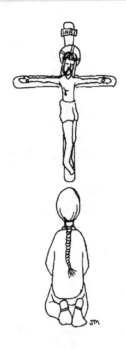

"When you pray, say: 'Father . . .' " — LUKE 11:2

✗

You have received a spirit of adoption as sons,
by virtue of which we cry, "Abba! Father!"
— ROMANS 8:15

My Questions

⊚ What is a true and good prayer that is certain to please God our Father?

⊚ Should I buy one thousand prayer books?

⊚ Has Jesus written prayer books?

The Word of God

How strange it is that Jesus did not write any books! As far as we know from the Gospel accounts, He taught only one prayer to His disciples. When they saw Him praying, they also decided to pray! (Read Matthew 6:9-13.)

Because Jesus himself taught us only the Our Father prayer, don't we need to listen to it carefully and attentively, as the Virgin Mary did when she heard it for the first time? From that day onward, our Mother probably never ceased to pray the Our Father — which contains all the prayer we need — to please God, since Jesus gave it to us.

Prayer

My Prayer to God

So, with Jesus praying to His Father, we can say:

Our Father who art in heaven, hallowed be thy name; thy kingdom come; thy will be done on earth as it is in heaven. Give us this day our daily bread; and forgive us our trespasses as we forgive those who trespass against us; and lead us not into temptation, but deliver us from evil. Amen.

A Friend of Jesus

There once was a five-year-old boy who asked a monk: "What is God?"

This boy consecrated his whole life to seek an answer to this all-important question. He became a great doctor (or teacher) of the Church, and we know him today as *St. Thomas Aquinas.*

Would you also like to exercise your intelligence, not only to get good grades but also to discover who God is?

Chapter 3

"Our Father . . ."

"I praise you, Father, Lord of heaven and earth,
That you did hide these things from the wise and
prudent and did reveal them to little ones."
— LUKE 10:21

My Questions

◎ If the Father in heaven knows what is in our heart and mind, why do we pray?

◎ How can I understand the meaning of the seven petitions Jesus gave us to pray in the Our Father?

The Word of God

We pray as a response to God's love for us:

Behold what manner of love the Father has bestowed upon us, that we should be called children of God. . . . Beloved, now we are the children of God, and it has not yet appeared what we shall be. We know that, when he appears, we shall be like to him, for we shall see him just as he is. And everyone who has this hope in him makes himself holy, just as he also is holy. — 1 JOHN 3: 1, 2-3

Try to recite the Our Father slowly, with attention, closing your eyes. Your Father in heaven is listening to you. The seven petitions of this prayer are the best prayers you can address to Him because Jesus himself taught us this prayer.

Prayers

My Prayer to God

Yes, Lord, I now pray to you, not only as the Creator of my soul but also as the Father who gives me his own divine life in and through Jesus Christ. It was not enough for you to make me in your own image by the gift of your Spirit. As eternal Father, you never cease to love us, and me personally, with an infinite love, even when I, unfortunately, forget your existence and your love for me.

Thank you so much, Father. Amen.

My Prayer for Others

Lord Jesus Christ, we thank you for revealing to us that not only is God the most loving Father, but that we have the promise of seeing him and you one day, face-to-face, and that our joy will never end. We present now to your mercy all the children on earth and their parents who do not know this wonderful news.

Thank you, Lord. Amen.

A Friend of Jesus

"On entering Thérèse's cell one day, I was struck by her heavenly expression of recollection. Although she was sewing industriously, she seemed to be lost in profound

contemplation. When I inquired, 'What are you thinking about?' she replied, with tears in her eyes: 'I am meditating on the Our Father. It is so sweet to call God "Our Father"!'

"She loved God as a child loves his father, with outbursts of incredible tenderness. One day during her illness, when referring to him, she said, 'Papa' when she had meant to say 'God.' It seemed to her that we were smiling over her slip, and with much feeling she told us: 'Nevertheless, he is indeed my "Papa," and it is a consolation for my heart to be able to call him by that name!' "

— FROM *MY SISTER, SAINT THÉRÈSE,*
BY CÉLINE MARTIN

Chapter 4

"Who Art in Heaven . . ."

Praise the LORD from the heavens, praise him in the heights!
Praise him, all his angels, praise him all his host!
— PSALM 148:1

"Our Father, who art in heaven . . ."
— MATTHEW 6:9

My Questions

⊚ Since Jesus doesn't say "who art in the sky," what is meant by the word "heaven," where the Father is?

⊚ What passage of Holy Scripture may help us to understand better what Jesus means?

The Word of God

God is light. . . . God is love. — 1 JOHN 1:5; 4:8

"In my Father's house there are many mansions. Were it not so, I should have told you, because I go to prepare a place for you." — JOHN 14:2

Heaven is a way of being, according to the *Catechism of the Catholic Church*. It does not mean that God is far from us in distance but rather He is way above us because of His greatness. St. Augustine clarifies this teaching when he says:

"Our Father, who art in heaven" is rightly understood to mean that God is in the hearts of the just, as in his holy temple. At the same time, it means that those who pray should desire the one they invoke to dwell within them.

Finally, Jesus himself indicates to us how to make our heart "heaven" when He said:

"If anyone loves me, he will keep my word, and my Father will love him, and we will come to him and make our abode with him." — John 14:23

Therefore, you understand now that God the Father is with us on earth, because we have heaven in us if God dwells in our soul. What an amazing and wonderful reality to contemplate!

Prayer

My Prayer to God

Father, who mysteriously dwells in my soul, I am so happy to know that I don't need to wait until the death of my body to live with you, because you are in me, as you are in your temple. Therefore, I want to adore your holy presence in me and in others several times a day. I bless you for the gift of my being. I love you, Father of my life, natural and divine. Into your hands I commend my spirit. Amen.

A Friend of Jesus

"It seems to me that I have found heaven on earth, since heaven is God and God is in my soul. The day I understood this, everything became luminous in me, and I wish to tell this secret to those I love, discretely."

— Blessed Elizabeth of the Trinity

Chapter 5

"Hallowed Be Thy Name . . ."

In the name of the Father, and of the Son,
and of the Holy Spirit. Amen.
— THE SIGN OF THE CROSS

"I made known to them your name, and will make it
known, in order that the love with which you have loved
me may be in them, and I in them."
— JOHN 17:26

My Questions

- ⊚ Why do I always begin a prayer with the Sign of the Cross?
- ⊚ Why do I sign myself when I enter a church?
- ⊚ And why do I do it "In the name of the Father . . ."?

The Word of God

Jesus said to His disciples just after His resurrection on Easter *Sunday* (the day of the week when we especially gather at Mass to celebrate the good news):

> *"Go, therefore, and make disciples of all nations, baptizing them in the name of the Father, and of the Son, and of the Holy Spirit."* — MATTHEW 28:19

That is why — since your baptism in Jesus Christ — you always pray in the name of the three divine persons. In a very mysterious and invisible manner, the Holy Trinity has been dwelling in your soul since your baptism! Don't you think that we can now pray and say a thousand thank-yous to God, to Jesus, for the amazing gift of His divine life in our souls?

Prayers

My Prayer to God

Lord, I want to know you. Is your name "God" only? You answered Moses, who asked what your name was: "I AM WHO I AM" (Exodus 3:14).

But, Lord, I desire to discover much more deeply who you are. St. John wrote about you and revealed that "God is light" (1 John 1:5) and that "God is love" (1 John 4:8). Thank you, Jesus, for having made the name of your Father known in many ways. With you, Jesus, I pray with your own words: "Holy Father, keep in your name those whom you have given me, that they may be one even as we are" (John 17:11). Amen.

My Prayer for Others

Lord, I desire that all children of the world who have never heard your name may receive the chance to know you, the Creator of their being and their loving Father.

Thank you, Lord. Thank you, Mary, our Mother, for your motherly intercession. Amen.

A Friend of Jesus

"We ask God to hallow his name, which by its own holiness saves and makes holy all creation. . . . But we ask that this name of God should be hallowed in us through our actions.

For God's name is blessed when we live well, but is blasphemed when we live wickedly."

— St. Peter Chrysologus

Chapter 6

"Thy Kingdom Come . . ."

Behold, he comes with the clouds, and every
eye shall see him. — REVELATION 1:7

"It is True, I come quickly!" Amen! Come, Lord Jesus!
— REVELATION 22:20

My Questions

⊚ What is the kingdom that Jesus is speaking about?

⊚ If the kingdom of God is not the whole universe but something else, what kind of king is coming?

The Word of God

Jesus says in the Gospel of John (18:36-37):

"My kingdom is not of this world. If my kingdom were of this world, my followers would have fought that I might not be delivered to the Jews. But, as it is, my kingdom is not from here." Pilate therefore said to him, "You are then a king?" Jesus answered, "You say it; I am a king. This is why I was born, and why I have come into the world, to bear witness to the truth. Everyone who is of the truth hears my voice."

As the Word of God incarnate, Jesus is the King of the whole world. He said, "I am the way, and the truth, and the life" (John 14:6).

Isn't the kingdom God himself, who is "Light" and "Love" and who wants to reign in our hearts?

"Behold, I come quickly! And my reward is with me, to render to each one according to his works."

— REVELATION 22:12

Prayers

My Prayer to God

Lord, I know now that you do not want to reign over us like the general of an army, but as a loving Father. I know that you are in my soul each time I pray to you from the bottom of my heart. I know that you come to me and enlighten me when I listen to your words as the Virgin Mary did. I believe that you especially come into my soul when, well prepared, I receive your Eucharistic presence during the Holy Sacrifice of the Mass. But I most desire to see you return in your glory so that all people on earth will see you as you are. Please come soon, Lord Jesus. Amen.

My Prayer for Others

Lord, I do not want to forget to pray for all those who don't believe in you, so that they, too, can welcome you with joy when you return in your glory. Amen.

A Friend of Jesus

"Await Jesus' coming in union with the Virgin Mary who awaits him; always joyfully.

"Life is short, suffering doesn't last and is brief, but afterwards: Paradise! Paradise, Paradise! Therefore, courage." — St. Maximilian Kolbe

Chapter 7

"Thy Will Be Done on Earth as It Is in Heaven . . ."

"I do always the things that are pleasing to him."
— JOHN 8:29

"Not my will but yours be done."
— LUKE 22:42

My Questions

⊚ What does Jesus mean by "Not my will but yours be done"?

⊚ How can we know what God wants from us?

The Word of God

Jesus says in the Gospel of Matthew (7:21):

"Not everyone who says to me, 'Lord, Lord,' shall enter the kingdom of heaven; but he who does the will of my Father in heaven shall enter the kingdom of heaven."

Jesus made this very clear on the eve of His death, at the Last Supper, when He said to His twelve apostles and, therefore, to each one of us:

"A new commandment I give you, that you love one another: that as I have loved you, you also love one another. By this will all men know that you are my disciples, if you have love for one another."

— John 13:34-35

Prayers

My Prayer to God

Lord, I have to admit before you that ever since I was little, I have found it difficult to obey my parents and my teachers. So many times during the day I say or think, "I want this" or "I want that." If I don't get what I want, I become angry, grouchy, and I find myself in a bad mood. Lord, I need your help. Without your grace, I can do nothing. Please, Father, send me your invisible Spirit of love so that, like Jesus and Mary, I will always seek what pleases you in order to give you glory.

Thank you, Father. Amen.

My Prayer for Others

Lord, I am not the only one who has a hard time being obedient. Please send your Spirit of charity to my friends, and to all the children and adults who may not even seek to do your will or know you as the most loving Father.

Thank you, Lord. Amen.

A Friend of Jesus

"When God loves, he doesn't want anything else but to be loved; for he loves in order to be loved, knowing that with this love, those who will have loved him will be happy."

— St. Bernard of Clairvaux

Chapter 8

"Give Us This Day Our Daily Bread . . ."

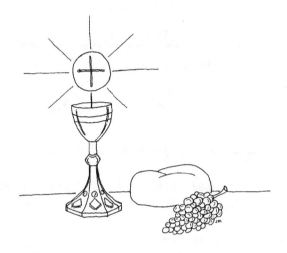

"Moses did not give you the bread from heaven,
but my Father gives you the true bread from heaven."
— JOHN 6:32

"I am the living bread that has come down from heaven.
If anyone eats of this bread he shall live forever."
— JOHN 6:51

My Questions

⦿ Why does Jesus teach us this petition asking for "our daily bread"?

⦿ Thanks to my parents, I receive my daily food. What bread does Jesus invite us to ask of God the Father?

The Word of God

People study and work a lot today, but we sometimes forget what Jesus said:

"Do not labor for the food that perishes, but for that which endures unto life everlasting, which the Son of Man will give you." — JOHN 6:27

"Not by bread alone does man live, but by every word that comes forth from the mouth of God." — MATTHEW 4:4

"And the Word was made flesh, and dwelt among us." — JOHN 1:14

You understand now that God, our Creator and good Father, gives food to all of us on earth. Therefore, Jesus invites us, the children of God, to ask His Father for this daily food. What is this necessary daily food? It is Jesus himself, His loving presence received during Mass in the

Sacrament of the Eucharist, after having received Him as the Living Word through the readings.

———————————— Prayers ————————————

My Prayer to God

Dear Father, full of trust in your infinite tenderness for me, a poor little child, I eagerly ask you to dispose my heart to listen to Jesus, your beloved Son, when I read the Gospel, and to listen to the Spirit of love when I pray. Increase in me the desire to receive the supreme sign of his love on earth, his Eucharistic presence, as the actual gift of his personal love for me.

Father, I want to say with Jesus: "My food is to do the will of him who sent me, to accomplish his work" (John 4:34). Amen.

My Prayer for Others

Jesus, when I pray with these words, "Give us this day our daily bread," I want to present to you all of the children, all of the people on earth who have not enough to eat every day, and those who have not yet discovered the gift of your love in the Eucharistic bread of your Body and Blood.

Thank you, Lord. Amen.

———————————— A Friend of Jesus ————————————

"When a child knows how to recognize the Eucharistic

bread from ordinary bread, when he has been instructed sufficiently, let us not worry about his age; the King of heaven must come and reign in his soul." — St. John Bosco

Chapter 9

@

"And Forgive Us Our Trespasses as We Forgive Those Who Trespass Against Us . . ."

"Lord, how often shall my brother sin against me, and I forgive him? Up to seven times?" Jesus said to him, "I do not say to you seven times, but seventy times seven."
— MATTHEW 18:21-22

✝

"Love your enemies, do good to those who hate you, and pray for those who persecute you, so that you may be children of your Father in heaven."
— MATTHEW 5:44-45

My Questions

- If someone in my own family or at school hurts me or someone I love, how can Jesus expect me to forgive, and to forgive him or her many times? Is it impossible?
- When I see people who are mean, who do evil things, or who attack the Catholic Church, the pope, and us Christians, how is it possible to love them and to forgive them?
- When God our Father forgives me, does He do it only if I forgive others first?

The Word of God

Yes, without special help from God, it is impossible to always forgive. That is why Jesus said: "Without me you can do nothing" (John 15:5).

That is why we absolutely need to pray every day, so as to love others with Jesus' heart, asking to receive His spirit of divine love. Jesus has told us:

"Ask, and it shall be given you; seek and you shall find; knock, and it shall be opened to you. For everyone who asks, receives; and he who seeks, finds; and to him who knocks, it shall be opened." — Matthew 7:7-8

St. John tells us:

If anyone says, "I love God," and hates his brother, he is a liar. For how can he who does not love his brother [or his sister], whom he sees, love God, whom he does not see?
— 1 JOHN 4:20

Prayers

My Prayer to God

Father, I come before you as a very weak child who sometimes has a real hard time forgiving others. I strongly desire to carry out Jesus' last commandment: "As I have loved you, you also love one another" (John 13:34). So as to be a true witness of his loving presence in my own family and at school, help me to look at others not with my own eyes, but with your merciful eyes, since you never cease to forgive our sins.

Thank you, dear Father. Amen.

My Prayer for Others

Good and merciful Father, I beg you that my firm intention to forgive others seventy times seven — always, like you do toward me — will change their hearts as well. May they experience the joy of forgiving and the joy of knowing that you will never cease loving them, even in all their failings and weaknesses.

Thank you, dear Father. Amen.

Act of Contrition

O my God, I am heartily sorry for having offended you. I detest all my sins because I dread the loss of heaven and the pains of hell.

But most of all because they offend you, my God, who are all good and deserving of all my love.

I firmly resolve, with the help of your grace, to sin no more and to avoid the near occasions of sin. Amen.

A Friend of Jesus

"I will never speak against my neighbor again; I will always try to excuse him [or her]."

— BLESSED ELIZABETH OF THE TRINITY

Chapter 10

༝༚༝

"And Lead Us Not Into Temptation, But Deliver Us From Evil. Amen."

"God is faithful, and he will not let you be tempted beyond
your strength, but with the temptation will also provide
the way of escape, that you may be able to endure it."
— 1 CORINTHIANS 10:13; RSV

My Questions

⊚ Why did Jesus say, "And lead us not into temptation," as if God could lead us into it?

⊚ How do we know that the various temptations we
have every day are not necessarily sins?

⊚ Did the devil — Satan — try to tempt Jesus? If yes,
how does Jesus help us today to be victorious when
we are tempted?

The Word of God

As you know, "God is love." He doesn't want His
children to be forced to depend on Him. So, He didn't
"lead" Adam and Eve, our first parents on earth, into
temptation. He let them exercise their free will to choose
to love their Creator and Father. He put them to the test:

*"You may freely eat of every tree of the garden; but of the
tree of the knowledge of good and evil you shall not eat, for
in the day that you eat of it you shall die."*

— GENESIS 2:16-17

As you know, they disobeyed God, their Father.
Disobedience is always a consequence of pride. When
we refuse to obey, or refuse to listen to our parents or to
our teacher, then we know that we sin out of pride.

Do you want to know how to resist temptations? Read in Chapter 4 of the Gospel of Matthew and see how Jesus was victorious over Satan.

Remember: If you don't *consent* to a temptation, you don't sin, and Jesus and Mary are very happy with you! Jesus gives us the secret to be victorious:

"Watch and pray, that you may not enter into temptation."
— MATTHEW 26:41

Prayers

My Prayer to God
Lord, I ask for your help when I am tempted to disobey, to do what I want when I know it is not good for me. Send me your Spirit of love and truth to strengthen my will when I am tempted to lie, to cheat at school, or to be mean toward my brothers, sisters, friends, or classmates.

I know, Lord, that if you didn't allow me to be tempted every day, I would not have opportunities to grow in prayer and trust in you — and I would not experience the joy of victory over evil.

Thank you, Father, for your help. Amen.

My Prayer for Others
Lord, many people on earth, many children who don't know Jesus and you, live in dependence on the devil, who plays tricks on them, just as he does with me at times.

Please listen to my prayer for them, and fill them with your light and your love. Amen.

Prayer to St. Michael the Archangel

St. Michael the Archangel, defend us in battle, be our defense against the wickedness and snares of the devil. May God rebuke him, we humbly pray; and do you, O Prince of the heavenly host, by the power of God, thrust into hell Satan and the other evil spirits who prowl about the world for the ruin of souls. Amen.

A Friend of Jesus

"Prayer does the most in our battle with temptations."

— St. Maximilian Kolbe

PART TWO

Each Day in Your Presence, Lord

"The hour is coming, and is now here, when the true
worshipers will worship the Father in spirit and in
truth. For the Father also seeks such to worship him.
God is spirit, and they who worship him must worship
in spirit and in truth."
— JOHN 4:23-24

Chapter 11

With You, Mary, I Wake Up

"HaiL, fuLL of grace. . . ." — LUKE 1:28

———————— My Questions ————————

⚜ If I want to show God that I truly desire to live every minute of the day He gives me in His holy presence, when do I start praying, and how?

⚜ Can Mary, Mother of Jesus and my Mother, help me?

The Word of God

If you open your Bible to the Book of Psalms that Mary, Joseph, and Jesus prayed in their house at Nazareth, you, too, can pray the prayers as they did, like these:

Let me hear in the morning of your steadfast love, for in you I put my trust. — PSALM 143:8

O God, you are my God, I seek you, my soul thirsts for you. — PSALM 63:1

"As a [deer] longs for flowing streams, so longs my soul for you, O God. My soul thirsts for God, for the living God. When shall I come and behold the face of God?" — PSALM 42:1-2

If you wish to keep expressing your desire for God during the day, you can memorize the words of these psalms that are directly inspired by the Holy Spirit. The Virgin Mary, because she treasured the word of God in her heart, certainly knew these psalms by heart because she loved to pray them. That's why she can help you to pray them as she did. She is our Mother, and she wants you to pray with her when you wake up, to adore God and praise Him first thing in the morning!

Prayers

My Prayer to God

Thank you, Lord, for giving me another day to love you. Before taking my shower and eating my breakfast, I want to recollect myself in your holy presence. At the very beginning of my day, I bow down before you at the foot of my bed, eyes closed, believing in your invisible presence in my soul. I adore you, my Creator and Father, and want to please you in absolutely everything I will do and say this day. With the heart of Mary, the Mother you gave me through Jesus your Son, I will love you today with all my heart.

Thank you, Father. Amen.

My Prayer for Others

Dear Father, I entrust to you today my parents (who do so much for me), my brothers and sisters, and all those children and adults I am going to meet today. Amen.

A Friend of Jesus

"A soul united to Jesus is a living smile that shines forth and gives him to others."

— Blessed Elizabeth of the Trinity

Chapter 12

🌀

Help Me, My Guardian Angel!

For he will give his angels charge of you to guard you in all
your ways. On their hands they will bear you up, lest you
dash your foot against a stone.
— PSALM 91:11-12

My Questions

⊚ Is it true that angels exist? It seems that many people don't believe in them at all, as if it were ridiculous to believe in such things. What is true about them?

⊚ If we can pray to angels, what can we ask them?

The Word of God

In the Gospel of Matthew, we see what Jesus himself reveals about guardian angels:

"See that you do not despise one of these little ones; for I tell you, their angels in heaven always behold the face of my Father in heaven." — MATTHEW 18:10

You can be certain that you have received a guardian angel, a pure spirit, from God, from the moment of your birth. Why? Because God is a loving Father who loves us infinitely and protects us from forgetting His presence throughout the day.

If you read the whole Bible, one or two pages every evening, you will see how many times angels have protected and prayed for the children of God. They help us to always be in perfect communion with God and His will. The Book of Psalms includes the following verse:

The angel of the LORD encamps around those who fear him, and delivers them. — PSALM 34:7

"Fear him," in this sense, means those who respect and adore Him. Why should we pray to angels? Because they can *intercede* for us, meaning that they present our prayers before God. You can read about them in the Book of Tobit:

"I am Raphael, one of the seven holy angels who present the prayers of the saints and enter into the presence of the glory of the Holy One." — TOBIT 12:15

Prayers

Prayer to My Guardian Angel
Angel of God, my guardian dear, to whom God's love commits me here, ever this day be at my side, to light and guard, to rule and guide. Amen.

(Thank you, Lord, for having given me such a strong protector for my soul. Amen.)

My Prayer for Others
O my God, I pray for children and adults who still don't know how good a Father you are, who don't know that they have received a guardian angel from you. Please reveal this to them.

Thank you, good Father. Amen.

A Friend of Jesus

"Beside each believer stands an angel as protector and shepherd leading him to life."

— St. Basil

Chapter 13

When and Where to Pray?

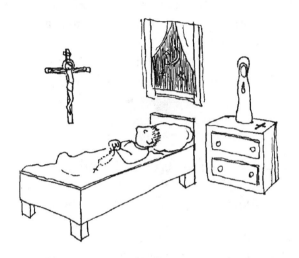

And rising up long before daybreak, Jesus went out and
departed into a desert place, and there he prayed.
— MARK 1:35

"Watch, then, praying at all times."
— LUKE 21:36

My Questions

⊚ What way of praying is pleasing to God, to Jesus? It seems that there are so many ways to pray and so many prayers!

⊚ Do I need to be at church to pray? When I pray, do I need to be completely alone with God?

The Word of God

Listen to Jesus responding to your questions:

"But when you pray, go into your room and shut the door and pray to your Father who is in secret; and your Father who sees in secret will reward you."

— MATTHEW 6:6; RSV

Does "room" mean the room where we sleep? Or is Jesus referring to another "room," maybe the interior room of our heart? Of course, it's good to have a little prayer corner in your room, with a crucifix and an image or a statue of Mary, our Mother; but Jesus also invites us to pray everywhere, to recollect anytime in spirit:

"The hour is coming, and is now here, when the true worshipers will worship the Father in spirit and in truth.

For the Father also seeks such to worship him. God is spirit, and they who worship him must worship in spirit and in truth." — JOHN 4:23-24

So you can talk to God, and also adore Him, with many acts of interior and silent adoration throughout the day!

Prayers

My Prayer to God

O my God, I want to believe in your holy presence in my soul and in the souls of others. I want to adore you, to trust you, to love you at each moment of the day, wherever I may be and whatever I may be doing. Amen.

My Prayer for Others

Father, I beg pardon for those who do not want to seek you and to adore you as their Creator and loving Father, and for those who don't put their trust in you and don't love you with their whole heart. Amen.

A Friend of Jesus

"You must build like me a little cell inside your soul; you'll believe that the good Lord is there and you'll enter in it."
— BLESSED ELIZABETH OF THE TRINITY

Chapter 14

On the Way to School

"I am The way, and The TruTh, and The Life."
— JOHN 14:6

My QuesTion

⑥ How can I pray in the morning when I am on my
way to school, often rushing and looking over my
homework?

The Word of God

When you are on the way to school, you can praise the Lord with some verses, such as these:

It is good to give thanks to the LORD, to sing praises to your name, O Most High; to declare your steadfast love in the morning, and your faithfulness by night.
— PSALM 92:1-2

O give thanks to the LORD, call on his name, make known his deeds among the peoples! Sing to him, sing praises to him, tell of all his wonderful works! Glory in his holy name; let the hearts of those who seek the LORD rejoice! Seek the LORD and his strength, seek his presence continually!
— PSALM 105:1-4

By praying these short verses from the psalms each day, your soul will become like the souls of Mary and Joseph when they were praying in Nazareth, filled with praise and joy.

Prayers

My Prayer to God

Lord, on my way to school I don't want to forget your loving gaze upon me and your holy presence. I don't want to let my mind be so worried about school and tests that I forget to think about you. I want to present to you, through the prayer of Mary, my Mother, all my classmates (whom you love infinitely) and my teachers as well. Fill our principal with wisdom to run the school as you wish, for the benefit of all those who work there.

Thank you, Father. Amen.

My Prayer for Others

I also want to pray for those who leave their home with a heavy heart this morning, and for those who have to stay at home because they are sick. Console them and strengthen them by your loving presence, dear Lord. For them I offer a decade of the Rosary. Amen.

—————— A Friend of Jesus ——————

Prayer of Abandonment

"Father, I abandon myself into your hands; do with me what you will.

"Whatever you may do, I thank you; I am ready for all, I accept all.

"Let only your will be done in me, and in all your creatures.

"I wish no more than this, O Lord.

"Into your hands I commend my soul; I offer it to you with all the love of my heart, for I love you, Lord, and so need to give myself,

"To surrender myself into your hands, without reserve, and with boundless confidence —

"For you are my Father!"

— VENERABLE CHARLES DE FOUCAULD

Chapter 15

At School . . . in Your Presence

Make me to know your ways, O LORD;
Teach me your paths. Lead me in your truth,
and teach me.
— PSALM 25:4-5

My Question

@ I know that going to school is necessary in order to learn, to someday get a job, and to be able to support a family. But in the eyes of God, should I not also acquire another kind of knowledge superior to all human ones — that is, knowledge about Him?

The Word of God

If obtaining good grades and a good job is the only reason we work hard, it is sad indeed! Like the great and wise King Solomon, let us ask God to fill our minds with His wisdom:

I prayed, and understanding was given me; I called upon God, and the spirit of wisdom came to me. — WISDOM 7:7

Those who get [wisdom] obtain friendship with God.
— WISDOM 7:14

I perceived that I would not possess wisdom unless God gave [it] to me. — WISDOM 8:21

Jesus himself — who is the Incarnate Wisdom — reveals to us what true, good work He expects from us:

"Do not labor for the food that perishes, but for that which endures unto life everlasting, which the Son of Man will give you." — JOHN 6:27

If you ask Jesus, "What are we to do so that we may perform the works of God?" He'll reply:

"This is the work of God, that you believe in him whom he has sent." — JOHN 6:29

Prayers

My Prayer to God

O my God and Creator of my soul, you gave me an intelligence to learn about the universe you created for us, your children. I know that going to school and doing my best are pleasing to you. But beyond getting good grades, I want to learn about you because you are our Father, whom we'll see face-to-face after we die. Please, increase in me the desire to know you and to love you. Also, infuse in my soul your divine love so that I can love my classmates and my teachers as you love them.

Thank you, Father. Amen.

My Prayer for Others

Lord, I present to you all the students of my school and all those who work there. I especially pray for some of my classmates who seem to be sad and who don't succeed well at school, maybe because of family problems. Please, Lord, give to all of us a spirit of loving compassion so that your presence will be felt in the whole school.

Thank you, Lord. Amen.

A Friend of Jesus

"Vain is knowledge that doesn't lead to love."

— St. Thomas Aquinas

Chapter 16

After School . . . My Visits to Jesus

I was glad when they said to me,
"Let us go to the house of the LORD."
— PSALM 122:1

My Questions

ⓖ After school, why is it good to visit the church before going home?

ⓖ Isn't Sunday the only day that Catholics have to go to church for Mass?

The Word of God

Jesus never stops loving you when you are at school! He continually tells you:

"As the Father has loved me, I also have loved you. Abide in my love." — JOHN 15:9

He died on the cross for us! Isn't it good, every day, to pay a visit to Him — as we do for our best friend — and keep repeating to Him several times the words of St. Peter:

"Lord, you know all things, you know that I love you." — JOHN 21:17

Also, in case you had a fight with your classmates or said mean things to some of them, remember what St. John wrote:

If anyone says, "I love God," and hates his brother, he is a liar. . . . And this commandment we have from him, that he who loves God should love his brother also.

— 1 JOHN 4:20, 21

Prayers

My Prayer to God

O my God and loving Father, now that school is over, I want to visit you in church to offer you my studies and to adore you for a few minutes. If I have not pleased you during class or in my relations with my classmates and teachers, I am sorry. On my way home now, I ask you to fill my heart with love so as to be a peacemaker in my family, filled with joy.

I ask you the same thing for my parents and for my brothers and sisters so that we will spend a peaceful evening as a family that lives in your holy presence.

Thank you, Lord. Amen.

My Prayer for Others

Jesus, I noticed that some of my classmates were not very joyful today. Please fill them with your Spirit of love so that whatever their problems may be, you will reveal to them your hidden presence in their souls and your infinite love for them.

Thank you, Lord. Amen.

A Friend of Jesus

"Eucharistic piety should be centered above all on the celebration of the Lord's supper, which perpetuates the pouring out of his love on the cross. But it has a logical prolongation . . . in the adoration of Christ in this divine sacrament, in the visit to the Blessed Sacrament, in prayer beside the tabernacle. . . . Jesus waits for us in this Sacrament of Love." — POPE JOHN PAUL II

Chapter 17

Before Homework, Playing, and Watching TV

Whatever you do in word or in work, do all
in the name of the Lord Jesus, giving thanks
to God the Father through him.
— COLOSSIANS 3:17

My Questions

⊚ Why should I pray before doing my homework? Does God care about it?

⊚ Why should I pray before using the computer or watching TV?

The Word of God

You know that God continues to love and watch over us in whatever we do and wherever we may be. We read in the Book of Psalms:

> *O Lord, . . . you know when I sit down and when I rise up; you discern my thoughts from afar. . . . Even before a word is on my tongue . . . , O Lord, you know it altogether. You [encircle] me behind and before, and lay your hand upon me.* — Psalm 139:1, 2, 4-5

We can pray to keep our eyes and mind always pure:

> *I will walk with integrity of heart within my house; I will not set before my eyes anything that is base.*
> — Psalm 101:2-3

Prayers

My Prayer Before Homework

Jesus, you worked with Joseph every day, but always in your Father's holy presence. I present my homework to you. Give me the grace to study with attention and to always search for what is true knowledge, helpful for my life on earth.

Thank you, Lord. Amen.

My Prayer Before Playing

Lord, now that I have finished my homework and helped my parents, I offer you my free time. May I use it to play in a good and peaceful way, alone or with my brothers and sisters, in your fatherly presence. Amen.

Prayer Before Using the Computer or Watching TV

Jesus and Mary, you see how many of us watch TV and use the computer every day for our homework, to play games, and to send e-mails.

Please help me not to become enslaved by it. Help me to use it only for what is good. To this end, I place a little crucifix on top of the computer and an image of you, Mary. I trust you, Mother, that you will help me not to watch bad movies or commercials.

Thank you, Jesus and Mary, for your protection. Amen.

A Friend of Jesus

"Have fun but don't offend God."   — St. Philip Neri

Chapter 18

Sports? Not Without You, Jesus!

"Where Two or Three are gathered Together for
my sake, There am I in The midST of Them."
— MATTHEW 18:20

———————— My QuesTions ————————

⑥ Many of us children like sports more than school-
work. Jesus didn't say anything about sports. How
can Christian children, who want to please God, find
something about it in the Bible?

◎ What do some friends of Jesus have to say about sports?

————————— The Word of God —————————

See how St. Paul can help us give sports a proper place in our lives:

> *Do you not know that those who run in a race, all indeed run, but one receives the prize? So run as to obtain it. And everyone in a contest abstains from all things — and they indeed to receive a perishable crown, but we an imperishable.* — 1 CORINTHIANS 9:24-25

So imagine what would happen to our souls, to our prayer times in the presence of Our Lord, if we were spending many hours each week playing sports. The risk is to compete for our own glory and to fall into the sin of vanity! But playing sports in a healthy way with friends, without feeling bad if we lose a game, is certainly good.

————————— Prayers —————————

My Prayer to God

O my God, I believe that you created my soul united to a body that is not made to do great physical feats but to be a

*sacred dwelling for your holy presence, especially when I
receive you in the Holy Eucharist. I want to thank you for the
dignity of my body, which is the temple of the Holy Spirit. I
am sorry that I forget your presence at times. Whatever fun I
may have in sports, I promise that I will try to set aside time
to pray every day.*

Thank you, God, for the gift of my body. Amen.

My Prayer for Others

*O my God, I present to you all the children and adults who
play sports more for their own glory than to relax and have a
good time. I pray for those whose lives are so overly focused on
sports that they don't think about your existence and don't
know how much you love them. Amen.*

A Friend of Jesus

*"Beloved children . . . sports, provided it is understood in a
Christian sense, is a good school for that great contest
which is our earthly life, whose goals are the perfection of
the soul, the reward of eternal happiness, the unfading
glory of the saints. Of that more lofty contest, sports is
merely a faint image, but what differences there are between
the two!"* — POPE PIUS XII

Chapter 19

⌇⌇⌇

Before and After Meals

ALL who believed . . . took their food with
gladness and simplicity of heart, praising God.
— ACTS 2:44, 46-47

My Questions

⊚ Why do we pray before meals?
⊚ Did Joseph, Mary, and Jesus pray at mealtime, too?

The Word of God

If your parents provide food for you, God is the first food provider. We read in the Book of Genesis:

God said, "Behold, I have given you every plant yielding seed which is upon the face of all the earth, and every tree with seed in its fruit; you shall have them for food."
— GENESIS 1:29

After the Flood, Scripture says this about animal flesh as food:

God blessed Noah and his sons and said to them, ". . . Every moving thing that lives shall be food for you; and as I gave you the green plants, I give you everything."
— GENESIS 9:1, 3

Therefore, Joseph, Mary, and Jesus, as prayerful Jews, knew the love the Father-Creator has for us, praised Him before each meal, and thanked Him afterward. Like them, you can praise the Lord with a few verses from the Book of Psalms found in "My Prayers to God."

Prayers

My Prayers to God (with my family too!)

Scripture Passages

*Bless the LORD, O my soul! O LORD my God, you are very
great!* — PSALM 104:1

*You do cause the grass to grow for the cattle, and plants for
man to cultivate, that he may bring forth food from the
earth, and wine to gladden the heart of man.*
— PSALM 104:14-15

*I will sing to the LORD as long as I live; I will sing praise to
my God while I have being.* — PSALM 104:33

Prayer Before Meals

*Bless us, O Lord, and these thy gifts, which we are about
to receive from thy bounty. Through Christ our Lord. (And we
pray for those who have nothing to eat.) Amen.*

Prayer After Meals

*We bless you, Father, for your goodness in providing food
that sustains our bodies. May we now use it to carry out your
will during the rest of this day, especially by loving one
another in Christ. Amen.*

A Friend of Jesus

"Therefore, whether you eat or drink, or do anything else, do all for the glory of God."

— St. Paul (1 Corinthians 10:31)

Chapter 20

Before Going to Bed

"Our Father Who art in heaven. . . ."
— MATTHEW 6:9

"Hail, full of grace. . . ."
— LUKE 1:28

My QuesTions

⑥ Why is it so important to pray before going to bed?

⑥ What should be included in this last prayer time of
the day?

The Word of God

At the end of the day, it is very important never to
forget to offer our day to our heavenly Father in an
attitude of profound respect and adoration. Why?
Because the reason He allows us to live on earth every
day is to give Him glory and love, as Jesus did.

You may say tonight (as Jesus did when He prayed to
the Father):

*"I have glorified you on earth; I have accomplished the
work that you have given me to do."* — JOHN 17:4

And you may start praying with the words of Psalm
141:1-2:

*I call upon you, O LORD; make haste to me! Give ear to my
voice when I call to you! Let my prayer be counted like
incense before you, and the lifting up of my hands as an
evening sacrifice!*

Prayers

My Prayer to God

Father, Son, and Holy Spirit, you who are one God in three divine persons, at the end of this day I adore you and place myself in your holy presence. Kneeling before you as your little creature and beloved child, I want, first of all, to say THANK YOU for being such an amazingly loving Father who keeps me in existence at each second out of a pure, freely-given love. I also want to beg pardon for my lack of love toward you and my neighbor today (family member or class-mate) and beg you to forgive me in your mercy. And because, as St. Peter said, "You know that I love you" (John 21:17), I want to say the same, and I can truly say: In God alone is my soul at rest (read Psalm 62:1). Amen.

My Prayer for Others

Lord, I beg your pardon for those who do not adore, believe, and hope in you, or love or seek you. Amen.

A Friend of Jesus

"At the end of our life we will be judged on our love."
— St. John of the Cross

PART THREE

I Pray With You, My Mother Church

ALL These wiTh one mind conTinued
STeadfasTly in prayer wiTh The women and Mary,
The moTher of Jesus, and wiTh his breThren.
— ACTS 1:14

Chapter 21

Never Alone When I Pray!

You have received a spirit of adoption as sons,
by virtue of which we cry, "Abba! Father!"
— ROMANS 8:15

My Questions

◎ Sometimes I feel very alone when I try to pray. Are we really alone when we pray?

◎ Is it only at church that we are invited to pray?

The Word of God

Jesus wanted a Church to exist — among many other reasons — to gather all of the children of God into one family, to live together in faith, hope, and charity. Jesus said to St. Peter, the first pope:

> *"I say to you, you are Peter, and upon this rock I will build my Church, and the gates of hell shall not prevail against it. And I will give you the keys of the kingdom of heaven."*
> — MATTHEW 16:18-19

If the apostle Peter was chosen to be the first pope in order to maintain the unity of faith within the Church of Jesus Christ, we also pray together "through him, with him, in him, in the unity of the Holy Spirit" in order to remain one in love. Our Mother Mary has always been present, since the very beginning two thousand years ago:

All these with one mind continued steadfastly in prayer with the women and Mary, the mother of Jesus, and with his brethren. — ACTS 1:14

Thus, you are never alone when you pray, whether in your room, on the way to school, or anywhere, because "we, the many, are one body in Christ" (Romans 12:5).

Prayers

My Prayer to God

Thank you, Father, for the gift of the Immaculate Mary, Mother of your Son, Jesus, Mother of the One who is the head of the Church, and our Mother because we are "one body in Christ." Thank you for never letting us pray alone, because you give us the Holy Spirit to love you with the love that comes from you. Thank you for giving us a pope to maintain communion among us, your children, scattered all over the earth. Amen.

My Prayer for Others

Father, please send your Holy Spirit of truth and love into the souls of the millions of adults and children who have not received baptism in Jesus Christ your Son, who are not in communion with you, and may not understand the great mystery of your Church.

Thank you, Father. Amen.

A Friend of Jesus

"I want to be a daughter of the Church . . . and to pray for the Holy Father's intentions which I know embrace the whole universe." — St. Thérèse of Lisieux

Chapter 22

The Rosary: Contemplation of Jesus Christ

"I am Our Lady of The Rosary. I come To ask you To say
The Rosary every day and To change your Life."
— OUR LADY OF FÁTIMA, OcT. 13, 1917

"HaiL, full of grace, The Lord is wiTh you. BLessed
are you among women." — LUKE 1:28

The angeL said To her, "Do noT be afraid, Mary, for you
have found grace wiTh God. Behold, you shaLL conceive
in your womb and shaLL bring forTh a son; and you shaLL

call his name Jesus. He shall be great and shall be called
The Son of The Most High." — LUKE 1:30-32

My Questions

⊚ There are many beautiful prayers in the Catholic
Church. Why do so many popes and saints consider
the Rosary to be such an important prayer?

⊚ What is the connection between the Rosary and the
liturgical prayer of the Church, especially from
Advent to Easter?

The Word of God

*And a great sign appeared in heaven: a woman clothed with
the sun, and the moon was under her feet, and upon her
head a crown of twelve stars.* — REVELATION 12:1

Prayer

Meaning of the Rosary

Perhaps you have been praying the Rosary for years,
or perhaps not. Maybe you would like to understand
what a special prayer it is, a prayer that helps us on our

way to heaven, where "eye has not seen nor ear heard, nor has it entered into the heart of man, what things God has prepared for those who love him" (1 Corinthians 2:9)

No other creature on earth except the Virgin Mary, the Immaculate Conception, has contemplated the mystery of God so deeply. She miraculously conceived in her womb the Word of God, the second person of the Holy Trinity! Unimaginable, but true. The archangel Gabriel revealed it to Mary.

After having spent thirty-three years with Jesus, after having listened to His teachings attentively and prayed with Him until His death on the cross, who better than Mary can help us contemplate the face of our Lord and Savior, Jesus Christ? That is why Pope John Paul II, who added five new mysteries to the Holy Rosary, wrote: "To recite the Rosary is nothing other than to contemplate with Mary the face of Christ."

This is also what we do at every Mass!

How to Pray the Rosary

There is more than one way to pray the Rosary. For example, you can pray one or more decades at a time, or the whole Rosary. Don't say it too fast! Our Father is listening to you, and our Mother Mary is listening, too! They are attentive to you and to your prayer, even though you don't see them. So, in faith, believe in their hidden and holy presence.

Jesus was a child, just as you are now a child. Like you, He experienced not only joys but also pain. By meditating on these chief mysteries of His life, you can see how, from His childhood to His sacrifice on the cross, He never ceased revealing to us how much we are loved by God. The Rosary is a beautiful way to thank Him for His unceasing love and mercy for us. Pray it every day if you can!

Beginning
(The prayers of the Rosary are in Appendix D, starting on page 137.)

- Start with the Sign of the Cross.
- Pray the Apostles' Creed. (We profess the truths of our Catholic faith.)
- Pray one Our Father and three Hail Marys (for faith, hope, and love).
- Pray the Glory Be. (We give homage and adoration to God.)

Praying the Mysteries
- Announce the mystery and then pray one Our Father.
- Pray ten Hail Marys. (We think about the mystery as we pray.)
- Pray the Glory Be.
- Pray the Fátima Prayer. (This prayer was requested by Our Lady in 1917.)

After the Fifth Mystery
- Pray the Hail, Holy Queen.
- Pray the Concluding Rosary Prayer.
- Pray the Sign of the Cross.

The Mysteries of the Rosary
(Selections of Scripture passages are listed below, to help you meditate on these mysteries.)

The Joyful Mysteries
(Meditations on the secret of Christian joy.)

These mysteries are normally prayed on Mondays and Saturdays, but they may also be prayed on any day during the seasons of Advent and Christmas.

- The Annunciation to Mary (Luke 1:26-38)
- The Visitation of Mary (Luke 1:39-56)
- The Birth of Jesus (Luke 2:1-20)
- The Presentation of Jesus (Luke 2:22-38)
- The Finding of Jesus in the Temple (Luke 2:41-51)

The Mysteries of Light
(Meditations on Jesus, the "Light of the world," and on the kingdom of God present in His very person in our midst.)

These mysteries are normally prayed on Thursdays, but they may also be prayed on any day during the season of Ordinary Time.

- The Baptism of Jesus (Matthew 3:13-17 and John 1:29-34)
- The Wedding Feast at Cana (John 2:1-11)
- The Preaching of the Kingdom of God (Mark 1:14-15, Luke 4:43, and John 18:36-37)
- The Transfiguration of Jesus (Luke 9:28-36 and Matthew 17:1-8)
- The Institution of the Eucharist at the Last Supper (Luke 22:14-20 and Matthew 26:26-29)

The Sorrowful Mysteries
(Meditations on the high point of the revelation of God's infinite loving mercy for us — His sinful children — and of our salvation.)

These mysteries are normally prayed on Tuesdays and Fridays, but they may also be prayed on any day during the season of Lent and Holy Week.

- The Agony in the Garden (Matthew 26:36-46 and Luke 22:39-46)
- The Scourging of Jesus (Matthew 27:26 and John 19:1)
- The Crowning With Thorns (Matthew 27:29 and John 19:2)
- The Carrying of the Cross (Matthew 27:31-32 and Luke 23:26-32)
- The Crucifixion of Jesus (Matthew 27:33-56, Luke 23:33-49, and John 19:17-37)

The Glorious Mysteries

(Meditations on the mysteries lived, first of all, by Mary, our Mother, with great joy. The resurrection of Christ and the glorification of His human body fill us on earth with the joyful hope that after our own death we will enter into heaven and be with Jesus and Mary.)

These mysteries are normally prayed on Wednesdays and Sundays, but they may also be prayed on any day during the season of Easter.

- The Resurrection of Jesus (Matthew 28:1-10, Luke 24:1-12, and John 20:1-18)
- The Ascension of Jesus (Luke 24:50-53 and Acts 1:6-12)
- The Descent of the Holy Spirit at Pentecost (Acts 2:1-4)
- The Assumption of Mary (Psalm 45:10-15)
- The Coronation of Mary, Queen of Heaven and Earth (Revelation 12:1)

A Friend of Jesus

"Let us live as the Blessed Virgin lived: loving God only, desiring God only, trying to please God only, in all that we do."
                                                — St. John Vianney

Chapter 23

※

The Psalms:
Prayers of the Children of God

Ps 63 O God, you are my God

O Lord, open my Lips, and my mouth shall
[proclaim] your praise.
— PSALM 51:15

My Questions

- ✆ I thought that the people of Israel prayed the Book of Psalms before Jesus' time? Why do we still pray them today?
- ✆ What kind of prayer are the psalms?
- ✆ Can I pray them anytime during the day?

The Word of God

Read and learn these few meaningful verses from various psalms first and see if you discover some answers to your questions:

My soul thirsts for God, for the living God. When shall I come and behold the face of God? — PSALM 42:2

O God, you are my God, I seek you, my soul thirsts for you. — PSALM 63:1

O sing to the LORD a new song; sing to the LORD, all the earth. Sing to the LORD, bless his name." — PSALM 96:1-2

Know that the LORD is God! It is he that made us, and we are his; we are his people, and the sheep of his pasture. — PSALM 100:3

"Gladden the soul of your servant, for to you, O Lord, do I lift up my soul." — PSALM 86:4

If you open your Bible and read a few of the one hundred fifty psalms, you will see how meaningful it is to pray them, to pray for those who suffer. Sometimes you feel great, and then you can pray one of the psalms that praise God and thank Him. On another day, you may feel a bit down, so choose another psalm that expresses what you feel inside your heart. But always remember that we pray in communion with all of the children of God, for all people on earth, as Jesus and Mary did. The Holy Family prayed with the psalms in Nazareth!

Prayers

My Prayer to God

God, I bless you for giving us these one hundred fifty psalms that are the words inspired by your Holy Spirit. Please remind me to pray them as my Mother Mary did, with the same spirit of adoration and deep love for you. Amen.

My Prayer for Others

Lord, thinking of all people on earth who might not know how to pray or to love because they do not know you or because they suffer too much — and for all those who are sad, in prison, sick, or dying today — I want to cry out to you with faith and hope: "The ones whom you love are sick!"

Thank you, Lord, for listening to us. Amen.

A Friend of Jesus

"What is more pleasing than a psalm? David expresses it well: 'Praise the Lord, for a psalm is good. Let their praise of our God be with gladness and grace!' Yes, a psalm is a blessing on the lips of the people, praise of God. . . ."

— St. Ambrose

Chapter 24

Mass: The Greatest Act of Love

In this is love, not that we have loved God,
but that he has first loved us, and sent his Son as
an offering for our sins. Beloved, if God has so loved us,
we also ought to love one another.
— 1 JOHN 4:10-11

My Questions

⑥ I thought that Mass was just the celebration of the Last Supper. How can I understand that it is, in fact, the greatest prayer?

⑥ Also, many of us children are not very attentive during Mass, and we even get bored sometimes. How can we participate more and enter into the mystery of the Mass?

The Word of God

Once more, Jesus himself answers your questions and helps us understand how the Mass is the greatest act of love toward God the Father and toward us:

For God so loved the world that he gave his only-begotten Son, that those who believe in him may not perish, but may have life everlasting. — JOHN 3:16

Before the feast of the Passover, Jesus, knowing that the hour had come for him to pass out of this world to the Father, having loved his own who were in the world, loved them to the end. — JOHN 13:1

"This is my body, which is being given for you; do this in remembrance of me." In like manner he took also the cup after the supper, saying, "This cup is the new covenant in my blood, which shall be shed for you." — LUKE 22:19-20

"Father, into your hands I commend my Spirit." And having said this, he expired.   — LUKE 23:46

You now understand that if prayer basically consists in the lifting up of our soul to God, to be one with the Holy Trinity in love, then the sacrifice of Jesus on the cross that we celebrate during Mass is the most perfect and greatest prayer of all. As one body in Christ through baptism, we offer ourselves, body and soul, in Jesus, to God the Father in a unique sacrifice of love.

Dear child, if you understand this a little more, can we still say that Mass is boring?

Prayers

Let Us Pray With Jesus Himself

". . . that all may be one, even as you, Father, are in me and I in you; that they also may be one in us, that the world may believe that you have sent me. . . . Father, I will that where I am, they also whom you have given me may be with me; in order that they may behold my glory, which you have given me, because you have loved me before the creation of the world."   — JOHN 17:21, 24

Let Us Pray With the Whole Church

We come to you, Father, with praise and thanksgiving, through Jesus Christ your Son. Through him we ask you to accept and bless these gifts we offer you in sacrifice. We offer them for your holy catholic Church, watch over it, Lord, and guide it; grant it peace and unity throughout the world.

— EUCHARISTIC PRAYER I OF THE MASS

A Friend of Jesus

"Inasmuch as God has loved us infinitely and manifested his love by coming to earth in order to raise up, enlighten, and strengthen man by even submitting to the most shameful death to redeem him, we too should love him infinitely."

— ST. MAXIMILIAN KOLBE

Chapter 25

🌀

Mother Mary, Prepare My Heart for Mass

Now There were standing by The cross of Jesus
his mother and his mother's sister,
Mary of Cleophas, and Mary Magdalene.
— JOHN 19:25

My QuesTion

🌀 Why, along with a few faithful followers of Jesus, was St. John the only disciple present with Mary at Calvary when Jesus lived His final agony out of love for us?

The Word of God

When Jesus was arrested in the Garden of Gethsemane, it is written:

Then all the disciples left him and fled. — MATTHEW 26:56

You see, at that moment, the disciples' fear of being arrested, just as Jesus had been, prevented them from staying with Him, with the exception of John. Peter followed Jesus for a while, but then he also abandoned Him.

We need to be very close to Mary, protected by her when we are persecuted for the truth, as Jesus was. We are called to offer ourselves with Jesus at Mass, out of love for our heavenly Father.

Prayer

My Prayer to the Virgin Mary

Mother of mercy and love, who was given to me by Jesus on the cross, I don't want to go to Mass without you. Prepare my heart to go to church as if I were going with you and Jesus to Calvary. Although I am a poor sinner, I know that I am truly loved by God. Intercede for me, even though I am unworthy to receive the Body and Blood of your beloved Son. Present me to him so that, full of confidence toward you, my Mother and my Queen, I may receive my Lord in the holy temple of my body, as you did.

Thank you, dear Mother. Amen.

My Prayer for Others

On my way to Mass, I present to you, Mother of all compassion, all your children who are sick in body or in soul, those who are in prison, and those who are depressed or lonely. Present them to Jesus so that their sufferings, united to the sufferings of Jesus, may obtain everlasting life for them. Amen.

A Friend of Jesus

"A person unreservedly consecrated to the Immaculate knows that there is no better preparation for Holy Com-

munion than to take that act in union with the Virgin Mary. She knows how best to prepare our hearts, and we can be certain that we will deeply please Our Lord in manifesting the greatest possible love for him."

— St. Maximilian Kolbe

Chapter 26

Are You Sick and in Pain? Pray!

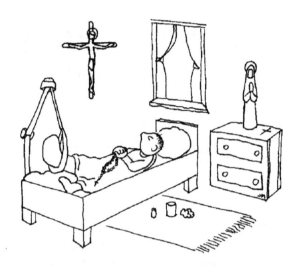

"Lord, behold, he whom you love is sick."
— JOHN 11:3

My Question

🌀 When I have a headache, or when I am sick in bed or
in the hospital and in pain, I usually complain and
don't think of other children and older people who
might be suffering more than I. How can I remain in
the presence of the Lord and pray when I'm sick?

The Word of God

In the Gospel, we read:

*Jesus went about all Galilee . . . healing every disease and
every sickness among the people. . . . They brought to him
all the sick suffering from various diseases and torments.*
— MATTHEW 4:23, 24

Then remember what the prophet Isaiah foretold
about Jesus:

Surely he has borne our griefs and carried our sorrows.
— ISAIAH 53:4

Don't forget that if we believe that Jesus is God, the
"Word made flesh," He revealed the depth of His love
for us by taking all the most intense sufferings into His

own Passion. His compassion toward all who suffer made Him say:

"I was sick and you visited me."— MATTHEW 25:36; RSV

Yet Jesus did not heal everyone. He healed a few to signify that He was the true physician — not so much of our bodies than of our souls filled with sins!

At Mass, offer Jesus your body and its pain in union with Him. You can do it even from your bed at home!

Prayers

My Prayer to God (based on Psalm 6:2-3)

Have mercy on me, Lord, I have no strength; Lord, heal me, my body is racked; my soul is racked with pain. Amen.

Another Prayer to God

Almighty and ever-living God, I come to you with faith and hope in the person of Jesus Christ, your Son. I pray to you, heavenly Doctor of my body and soul. If it is your will, please heal me. If in your divine wisdom you let me suffer for a time, so be it. But then give me the strength to offer it up in union with you, our Savior, who suffered for our sins.

I also offer to you my pain, a sacrifice for the sinners of this world, especially for those most in need of your grace.

Thank you, Lord. Amen.

A Friend of Jesus

"I cannot sleep, I am suffering too much, therefore, I pray. . . ."

"And what do you say to Jesus?"

"I don't tell him anything — I love him!"

— FROM A CONVERSATION WITH
ST. THÉRÈSE OF LISIEUX

Chapter 27

Enter Into Jesus' Prayer Before and During His Passion

"Father, if you are willing, remove this cup from me;
yet not my will but yours be done."
— LUKE 22:42

My Question

🌀 The Our Father is also called the Lord's Prayer. Is there another prayer that the Lord gave us?

The Word of God

If you read the four Gospels, you will realize how often Jesus prayed. His whole life was prayer — love of His Father and ceaseless intercession for us. But at the Last Supper with His disciples and before entering into His terrible Passion, He prayed to His Father and expressed the deep desires of His heart. I invite you to treasure that prayer of Jesus in your own heart:

"Father, the hour has come! Glorify your Son, that your Son may glorify you, even as you have given him power over all flesh, in order that to all you have given him, he may give everlasting life. Now this is everlasting life, that they may know you, the only true God, and him you have sent, Jesus Christ. I have glorified you on earth; I have accomplished the work that you have given me to do. And now do you, Father, glorify me with yourself, with the glory that I had with you before the world existed. . . . I am no longer in the world, but these are in the world, and I am coming to you. Holy Father, keep in your name those

*whom you have given me, that they may be one even as we
are."*   — JOHN 17:1-5, 11

(**A suggestion:** You may want to read and pray the other passages of this profound prayer in John 17, maybe a short passage every night.)

Prayers

Prayers of Jesus Crucified (Pray these often!)

"Father, forgive them, for they do not know what they are doing."   — LUKE 23:34

"My God, My God, why have you forsaken me?"   — MATTHEW 27:46

"I thirst."   — JOHN 19:28

"Father, into your hands I commend my spirit."   — LUKE 23:46

My Prayer to Jesus Crucified

My good and dear Savior, I kneel before you and ask you to deeply engrave upon my heart faith, hope, and charity. Contemplating your suffering through the wounds of your Passion, I begin to realize the seriousness of our sins and at the same time your infinite loving mercy for us. I firmly intend, with the help of your grace, to stop sinning in many ways that offend you, and to show you my love in loving my neighbor in whom you are hidden. Amen.

Sacrificial Prayer (from Fátima)

O my Jesus, I do this for love of you, for the conversion of poor sinners, and in reparation for offenses against the Immaculate Heart of Mary. Amen.

A Friend of Jesus

"You know, O my God, I have never desired anything but to love you, and I am ambitious for no other glory."
— St. Thérèse of Lisieux

Chapter 28

🌀

We Pray as One Body in Christ

Lord, look upon this sacrifice which you have given
to your Church; and by your Holy Spirit, gather all
who share this one bread and one cup into the one body
of Christ, a living sacrifice of praise.
— EUCHARISTIC PRAYER IV OF THE MASS

My Question

🌀 If Jesus prayed so earnestly for unity among all the children of God, when and where can we respond to His desires the most — by praying alone or in common?

The Word of God

Jesus sent the Holy Spirit upon the apostles and Mary in order to found His Church on them, so that they could pray together in one place, thereby manifesting this unity in Christ:

> *When the days of Pentecost were drawing to a close, they were all together in one place. . . . And they were all filled with the Holy Spirit.* — ACTS 2:1, 4

Also, you cannot receive the Bread of life, Jesus' Body and Blood, unless you actively take part in the Sacrifice of the Holy Mass (unless you are sick, of course):

> *They continued steadfastly in the teaching of the apostles and in the communion of the breaking of the bread and in the prayers.* — ACTS 2:42

So going to church and living the mystery of the Eucharist together is essential to our Christian life, to cooperate with Christ, with the full realization of communion among all Christians in love.

Prayers

A Few Prayers of the Mass
(Here is a short review of some parts of the Mass and some prayers we say or hear, for you to meditate on and use.)

1. Penitential Rite
(We prepare our hearts.)
I confess to almighty God, and to you, my brothers and sisters, that I have sinned through my own fault, in my thoughts and in my words, in what I have done and in what I have failed to do; and I ask Blessed Mary, ever virgin, all the angels and saints, and you, my brothers and sisters, to pray for me to the Lord our God.

2. Kyrie
(We beg for Christ's mercy.)
Lord, have mercy. . . .

3. Gloria
(We glorify God for His infinite love.)
Glory to God in the highest. . . .

4. Liturgy of the Word
(We listen to the Word of God — to the Gospel especially — and meditate on it as Mary did.)
Thanks be to God. . . . Praise to you, Lord Jesus Christ.

5. Offertory

(We offer gifts to God in the Offertory Prayer, which is prayed by the priest, but in the name of us all.)

Blessed are you, Lord, God of all creation. Through your goodness we have this bread to offer, which earth has given and human hands have made. It will become for us the bread of life.

6. Preface to the Eucharistic Prayer

(We give thanks in this prayer offered by the priest.)

Father, all powerful and ever-living God, we do well always and everywhere to give you thanks. . . .

7. Acclamation Before the Eucharistic Prayer

(We praise God before the central prayer leading to the consecration of the bread and wine, the Eucharistic miracle of the presence of Jesus on the altar. We kneel in respect during the Eucharistic Prayer.)

Holy, Holy, Holy Lord. . . .

8. Prayer After the Consecration

(We remember Jesus and His perfect offering to the Father.)

In memory of his death and resurrection, we offer you, Father, this life-giving bread, this saving cup . . . [from Eucharistic Prayer II].

9. Lord's Prayer

(We join in the prayer that is prayed by all of God's children, as members of His family and as the mystical body of Christ.)

Our Father. . . .

10. Lamb of God

(We pray as the consecrated bread and wine are prepared for Communion.)

Lamb of God, you take away the sins of the world, have mercy on us. . . .

11. Prayer Before Communion
(We ask God to heal us, trusting in His mercy and love.)
Lord, I am not worthy to receive you, but only say the word and I shall be healed.

(**A suggestion:** Using a missal — a book with Mass prayers — is an excellent way to be more attentive and to truly pray with the priest and the other people during Mass.)

A Friend of Jesus

"I am the child of the Church and the Church is a Queen. The heart of a child does not seek riches and glory. What the child asks for is love. She knows only one thing, to love you, O Jesus." — St. Thérèse of Lisieux

Chapter 29

Giving Thanks!

Give Thanks in all circumstances; for This is
The will of God in Christ Jesus for you.
— 1 THESSALONIANS 5:18; RSV

My Question

🌀 I learned that we pray and express our faith, hope, and love for God in many ways. What would be a good prayer of thanksgiving to God?

The Word of God

The Mother of the Church, Mary, inspired by the Holy Spirit, reveals to us her way of thanking God the Father for having chosen her as Mother of our Savior, Jesus Christ:

"My soul magnifies the Lord, and my spirit rejoices in God my Savior; because he has regarded the lowliness of his servant; for, behold, henceforth all generations shall call me blessed; because he who is mighty has done great things for me, and holy is his name; and his mercy is from generation to generation on those who fear him. He has shown might with his arm, he has scattered the proud in the conceit of their heart. He has put down the mighty from their thrones, and has exalted the lowly. He has filled the hungry with good things, and the rich he has sent away empty. He has given help to Israel, his servant, mindful of his mercy — even as he spoke to our fathers — to Abraham and to his posterity forever." — LUKE 1:46-55

Yes, it is a long prayer of thanksgiving! But if you pray with it along the years, it is like being one voice in prayer with our Mother! Is there a better prayer to thank God the Father for having sent us a Savior for our sins, which were depriving us of the happy vision of God?

Prayers

My Prayer to God

How can I thank you, Lord, for having made known to me, your child, your existence as Creator, your infinite love as Father, and my salvation in Jesus Christ, your Son, in whom I receive the hope to see you one day, face-to-face? As a way to thank you especially for the gift of faith in you, I want to often offer you these three prayers of faith, hope, and love:

An Act of Faith

O my God, I firmly believe that you are one God in three divine persons: Father, Son, and Holy Spirit. I believe that your divine Son became man and died for our sins, and that he will come to judge the living and the dead. I believe these and all the truths which the Holy Catholic Church teaches, because you revealed them, who can neither deceive nor be deceived. Amen.

An Act of Hope

O my God, relying on your infinite goodness and promises, I hope to obtain pardon of my sins, the help of your grace, and life everlasting, through the merits of Jesus Christ, my Lord and Redeemer. Amen.

An Act of Love

O my God, I love you above all things, with my whole heart and soul, because you are all good and worthy of all love. I love my neighbor as myself for the love of you. I forgive all who have injured me, and I ask pardon of all whom I have injured. Amen.

A Friend of Jesus

"Lord, Father all-powerful and ever-living God, I thank you, for even though I am a sinner, your unprofitable servant, not because of my worth, but in the kindness of your mercy, you have fed me with the precious Body and Blood of your Son, our Lord Jesus Christ."

— St. Thomas Aquinas

Chapter 30

Eucharistic Adoration for Children

"Let the children come to me, and do not hinder them;
for to such belongs the kingdom of heaven."
— MATTHEW 19:14; RSV

My Questions

- If I go to Mass at least every Sunday to celebrate Our Lord's resurrection, is it enough to make me a good Catholic?
- Why is spending time in silent adoration of Jesus in the Blessed Sacrament so important for many saints and strongly encouraged by the Catholic Church?

The Word of God

Now, we know by faith that Jesus is one in being with the Father. And in the Gospel, Jesus says in His prayer to the Father:

". . . that they may be one even as we are." — JOHN 17:11

So, by adoring Jesus in His Eucharistic presence, we also adore and honor the Father. Didn't Jesus invite us to stay with Him in order to dwell in Him?

"Wait here and watch with me." — MATTHEW 26:38

Also, remember that Jesus calls us His "friends," even though He is God:

"I have called you friends, because all things that I have heard from my Father I have made known to you."
— JOHN 15:15

We love to spend time with our best friend. Therefore, we have more reason to spend time, even fifteen minutes a day, before the tabernacle, adoring our God who is the person of Jesus and also our best friend!

Prayers

My Prayer to God

Lord, even if I am not always kneeling before you who are present in the tabernacle of our church, in my heart at least I want to adore you and to love you as the Creator of my being and Father of my soul. Amen.

My Prayer for Others

I adore you, Lord, and present to your divine mercy all the souls of those who do not yet recognize you as our Creator, as our Father, and, in Jesus, as our Savior.

A Friend of Jesus

"The Eucharist is the supreme proof of the love of Jesus. After this, there is nothing more but heaven itself."
— St. Peter Julian Eymard

Appendix A

For the Leader: One Possible Way of Leading a Children's Holy Hour

1. Have exposition of the Blessed Sacrament with incense. (It is best if the children are not in the pews but allowed instead to be on the floor at the foot of the altar.)

2. The priest says a few introductory words while kneeling before the Blessed Sacrament. Then follow with the first act of prostration for all, lasting just one to two minutes.

3. One decade of the Rosary is slowly recited with the intention of asking our Mother Mary to help us adore Jesus as she did.

4. During the next twenty minutes, alternate with prayerful short songs (and/or spiritually uplifting readings) and silence in which the children can be instructed to thank Jesus while looking at the Host.

5. The priest can sit on the steps facing the children as they also sit before the Eucharist. He then may share a short teaching or story that relates to the Eucharistic presence of Jesus.

6. Resume adoration with one song, followed by silent prostration for about five minutes.

7. Invite the children to offer Jesus their petitions.

8. Have Benediction and Divine Praises.

9. After reposition and a song of praise, the pilgrim statue of Mary is passed on to another family for the week. (See "Special Notes" below.)

Special Notes

- Don't be afraid to have moments of silence during the adoration time. It is important that the children experience times of silence, because these moments are of equal importance in the Holy Hour.

- If possible, it is very beneficial to have a priest available for the Sacrament of Reconciliation for the last half hour.

- A statue of Mary, a traveling pilgrim statue that goes home with a new family each week, has proven to be very fruitful. The family is encouraged to pray the Rosary in front of the statue the week it is in their home.

Appendix B

Prayers Before the Blessed Sacrament

Acts of Adoration

We adore you — here present in the Blessed Sacrament of the altar — where you wait day and night, to be our comfort while we look forward to your unveiled presence in heaven.

Jesus, our God, we adore you in all places where the Blessed Sacrament is reserved, especially where you are little honored, and where sins are committed against this sacrament of love.

Jesus, our God, we adore you for all time — past, present, and future — for every soul that ever was, is, or shall be created.

Jesus, our God, who for our sake has deigned to subject yourself to the humiliation of temptation, to the disloyalty and defection of friends, to the scorn of your enemies, we adore you.

Jesus, our God, who for us has endured the buffetings of your Passion — the scourging, the crown of thorns, the heavy weight of the cross — we adore you.

Jesus, our God, who for our salvation, and that of all mankind, was cruelly nailed to the cross, hung thereon for three long hours in bitter agony, we adore you.

Jesus, our God, who for love of us did institute this Blessed Sacrament and offer yourself daily for the sins of men, we adore you.

Jesus, I live for you. Jesus, I die for you. Jesus, I am yours in life and in death.

Meditation Before the Blessed Sacrament

"Let us live with God as a friend, let us make our faith a living faith in order to be in communion with him through everything, for that is what makes saints.

"We possess our heaven within us, since he who satisfies the hunger of the glorified in light of vision gives himself to us in faith and mystery, it is the same One; it seems to me that I have found my heaven on earth, since heaven is God and God is in my soul.

"The day I understood that, everything became clear to me. I would like to whisper this secret to those I love so they, too, might always cling to God through everything and so that this prayer of Christ might be fulfilled: 'Father, may they be made perfectly one.' "

— BLESSED ELIZABETH OF THE TRINITY

An Offering of Self

"Take, O Lord, into your hands my entire liberty, my memory, my understanding, and my will. All that I am and have, you have given me, and I surrender them to you, to be so disposed in accordance with your holy will.

Give me your love and your grace; with these I am rich enough and desire nothing more."

— ST. IGNATIUS OF LOYOLA

Angel's Prayer

O Most Holy Trinity, Father, Son, and Holy Spirit, I adore you profoundly. I offer you the most precious Body, Blood, Soul, and Divinity of Jesus Christ, present in all the tabernacles of the world, in reparation for the outrages, sacrileges, and indifference by which he is offended. By the infinite merits of the Sacred Heart of Jesus and the Immaculate Heart of Mary, I beg the conversion of poor sinners.

Eucharistic Prayer

Most Holy Trinity, I adore you! My God, My God, I love you in the Most Blessed Sacrament!

Appendix C

For Educators, Priests, and Youth Leaders

Why bring children before the Eucharistic Heart of Jesus? What does our Holy Father, Pope John Paul II, say about the importance of Eucharistic adoration?

I urge priests, religious, and lay people to continue and redouble their efforts to teach the younger generations the meaning and value of Eucharistic adoration and devotion. How will young people be able to know the Lord if they are not introduced to the mystery of his presence? . . . The Eucharistic mystery is in fact the "summit of evangelization" (Lumen Gentium, n. 28), for it is the most eminent testimony to Christ's resurrection. All interior life needs silence and intimacy with Christ in order to develop. This gradual familiarity with the Lord will enable certain young people to be involved in serving as acolytes and to take a more active part in Mass; for young boys, to be near the altar is also a privileged opportunity to hear Christ's call to follow him more radically in the priestly ministry.

— POPE JOHN PAUL II
(FROM THE VATICAN, MAY 28, 1996)

Appendix D

Prayers of the Rosary

Sign of the Cross
In the name of the Father, and of the Son, and of the Holy Spirit. Amen.

Apostles' Creed
I believe in God, the Father almighty, creator of heaven and earth; and in Jesus Christ, his only Son, our Lord; who was conceived by the Holy Spirit, born of the Virgin Mary, suffered under Pontius Pilate, was crucified, died, and was buried. He descended into hell; the third day he arose again from the dead. He ascended into heaven and sits at the right hand of God, the Father almighty; from thence he shall come to judge the living and the dead. I believe in the Holy Spirit, the holy catholic Church, the communion of saints, the forgiveness of sins, the resurrection of the body, and life everlasting. Amen.

Our Father
Our Father who art in heaven, hallowed be thy name; thy kingdom come; thy will be done on earth as it is in heaven. Give us this day our daily bread; and forgive us our trespasses as we forgive those who trespass against us; and lead us not into temptation, but deliver us from evil. Amen.

Hail Mary

Hail Mary, full of grace. The Lord is with thee. Blessed art thou among women, and blessed is the fruit of thy womb, Jesus. Holy Mary, Mother of God, pray for us sinners, now and at the hour of our death. Amen.

Glory Be

Glory be to the Father, and to the Son, and to the Holy Spirit. As it was in the beginning, is now, and ever shall be, world without end. Amen.

Fátima Prayer

O my Jesus, forgive us our sins, save us from the fires of hell, lead all souls to heaven, especially those who have most need of your mercy. Amen.

Hail, Holy Queen

Hail, holy Queen, Mother of Mercy, our life, our sweetness, and our hope. To thee do we cry, poor banished children of Eve; to thee do we send up our sighs, mourning, and weeping in this valley of tears. Turn then, most gracious advocate, thine eyes of mercy toward us, and after this, our exile, show unto us the blessed fruit of thy womb, Jesus. O clement, O loving, O sweet Virgin Mary.

V. Pray for us, O Holy Mother of God.

R. That we may be made worthy of the promises of Christ.

Concluding Rosary Prayer

O God, whose only begotten Son, by his life, death, and resurrection, has purchased for us the rewards of eternal life, grant, we beseech thee, that meditating upon these mysteries of the Most Holy Rosary of the Blessed

Virgin Mary, we may imitate what they contain and obtain what they promise, through the same Christ our Lord. Amen.

About The Author

Father Antoine Thomas is a native of France who is currently chaplain of the Newman Center at Bradley University in Peoria, Illinois. He is a member of the Congregation of St. John and has been a frequent guest on EWTN, which has also aired Father Antoine's programs for children that explain the Mass and Eucharistic adoration.

The author holds a child of God by a statue of Mary, our Mother

Our Sunday Visitor ...
Your Source for Discovering the Riches of the Catholic Faith

Our Sunday Visitor has an extensive line of materials for young children, teens, and adults. Our books, Bibles, pamphlets, CD-ROMs, audios, and videos are available in bookstores worldwide.

To receive a FREE full-line catalog or for more information, call **Our Sunday Visitor** at **1-800-348-2440, ext. 3**. Or write **Our Sunday Visitor** / 200 Noll Plaza / Huntington, IN 46750.

Please send me ___ A catalog
Please send me materials on:
___ Apologetics and catechetics
___ Prayer books
___ The family
___ Reference works
___ Heritage and the saints
___ The parish

Name _____
Address _____ Apt._____
City _____ State _____ Zip_____
Telephone ( ) _____

A39BBABP

Please send a friend ___ A catalog
Please send a friend materials on:
___ Apologetics and catechetics
___ Prayer books
___ The family
___ Reference works
___ Heritage and the saints
___ The parish

Name _____
Address _____ Apt._____
City _____ State _____ Zip_____
Telephone ( ) _____

A39BBABP

OurSundayVisitor

200 Noll Plaza, Huntington, IN 46750
Toll free: **1-800-348-2440**
Website: www.osv.com